ONE **HAPPY** **THOUGHT** AT A TIME: *30 Days* **TO A HAPPIER YOU**

ROCHELLE GAPERE

Cover Design and Layout: Yetunde Shorters - www.yetundeshorters.com
Author Photo: Sean O'Neill

For information regarding special discounts for bulk purchases of this book, for charitable donation, or for speaking engagements, please visit
www.rochellegapere.com
ISBN: 978-1-7320360-0-0
Published by Rochelle Gapere
Printed in the United States of America

Introduction

In June 2016, I spent an incredible two weeks in Southeast Asia, splitting my time between Singapore and Bali. I flew to Bali to attend the wedding of a dear friend at Alila Villas Uluwatu, one of the most beautiful places I have ever visited. Travel is one of the things that makes me happiest.

Like many people - eating different cuisines, meeting new people, learning about different cultures, and the excitement of new adventure attract me to travel. Where I believe I may be unique, however, is that I am as excited about the process of getting there as I am about the destination. The actual 'flying in the airplane part' of the whole experience is one I eagerly look forward to. I feel closest to God amidst the clouds. As a child, I insisted on the window seat because I wanted to *see* God. As an adult, sitting by the window while looking at the expansive sky and beautiful clouds causes me to *feel* God. That view is one of the things guaranteed to give me peace, and over the years has been partly responsible for my tens of thousands of airplane miles.

On June 17, 2016, as I embarked on the 17-hour journey back to Miami from Bali, by way of Narita, I did what I do on every flight – I wrote in my prayer journal. Here is a significant portion of what I wrote that day, *"Lord, thank you for your favor. Thank you for blessing me with adventures beyond what my mind has at times failed to conceptualize. As I head home to Miami, my heart is full and overflowing with gratitude. To date, I have done every single thing I have ever imagined doing as a single woman. I know now, without a shadow of a doubt, that I am ready to get married."*

It was a profound declaration for me – a person who believes that God will only bless me with the desires of my heart when I am ready and only when I have the capacity to handle the blessing. At the time, I was in a long-term relationship. Five years to be exact! And I *believed* wholeheartedly that my boyfriend would be my husband. I knew I wanted to get married one day, but I was never in a hurry. I figured, like everything else in my life, it would happen organically and in due season. Little did I know that my journal entry amidst the clouds that day would set in motion a chain of events that would threaten my happiness as I knew it!

Nine days after returning to Miami, my boyfriend and I had the 'mother of all arguments', which eventually led to our relationship's demise. It was completely unexpected. The shock, pain, and disappointment were profound. Few things, if any, have destabilized my happiness. This did! I have always been a happy person. I must admit that I can't remember a time in my life when I wasn't happy. It is something for which I am extremely grateful. I had an extremely happy childhood, filled with an abundance of love, affection, and attention. As I grew older, life had its disappointments, the usual ups and downs, but for the most part, I had great perspective throughout, and happiness flowed in and out of my life pretty seamlessly. The end of my long-term relationship was the first time I was able to pinpoint a period where my happiness was significantly impacted. To date, my breakup has been the biggest disappointment of my life. Happily, I can now say it has also been one of my greatest blessings.

I have always been a source of encouragement and unwavering support for my loved ones. Lost a job? Call Rochelle. Fighting illness? Call Rochelle. Best friend betrayed you? Call Rochelle. Whatever the issue was, friends and family knew they could call on me to give them honest, fair and loving advice, a shoulder to cry on, and support. It is true that you reap what you sow. In the most disappointing season of my life, I had some of those same friends and family members lovingly show up for me. I also reaped every single ounce of advice I had ever sown in the lives' of others by applying it to *myself.*

One happy thought at a time was birthed in that season. It wasn't called that then. I also had no idea at the time that my pain would be the stimulus to fulfilling one of my life's goals of becoming a published author. I will never forget the day when I packed the last of my belongings and drove away from the home my boyfriend and I had shared. I remember having a moment of crystal clarity where I made a promise to myself, *"You are going to leave the sadness and disappointment right here. If you take it with you, it would mean that the relationship has now gotten 5 years + 1 more day of your life."* I was **not** going to invest one more second of my precious time on that chapter of my life. I had the power of choice and I chose to move on. As difficult as I imagined it would be, I chose happiness.

The days that followed were not easy. In fact, they were filled with tons of angst, regret, fear, and disappointment. However, they were also filled with lots of hope, prayer, gratitude, faith, and the anticipation of a brighter future. I started extending the grace I had so lovingly extended to others to myself. Each day I would wake up with a mission: *Do one thing today that makes you happy.*

I awakened each day with a spirit of expectation. In the midst of the disappointment, knowing that I had to think about, and then follow through with one thing each day to make me happy, empowered me. A few days in, my energy started shifting. I knew some days would be harder than others, so I pre-planned my happiness. I made lists of things I could do to add happiness to my life if ever my spirit felt too heavy to do it. My lists included things such as: 1) go to the library and get lost in the aisles trying to find a new and interesting book; 2) listen to sermons by Bishop Joseph Walker III; 3) spend the day poolside with a great book; 4) talk to and laugh with Mummy on the phone; 5) dance to my favorite Soca songs; 6) go on a prayer walk, and more. The things on my list were simple, free, and easily accessible. But most importantly, they were things I knew without a shadow of a doubt would make me happy.

About 30 days in, I felt great! The more I infused my life with happiness, the happier I became. Of course, the disappointment and hurt still lingered and would creep up at unexpected times. But I was so well versed in my happiness practice that I was able to acknowledge the feelings, and then counteract them. Some days it would be as simple as having a sad thought pop in my head, then using that as a cue that it was time to turn on some music and dance! During that season, I spent a lot of time laughing at myself as I observed myself battling to preserve my happiness. It was such a special period in my life because I got to know myself on a deeper level. There were many days when my heart swelled with pride as I looked at my reflection in the mirror, and commended myself for choosing me, for choosing my happiness.

Eventually, I decided I was going to bring others along on my journey. It happened pretty organically too. One afternoon, I was lounging poolside at the Mondrian and posted my first *#RoRoLifeNugget* on Instagram. It was essentially a quote by me; one of the many quotes I had written in my prayer journal and then one or two paragraphs of encouraging words. I ended the entry with *#happinessis...* and included what happiness was to me in that moment.

I began to post more life nuggets, and a beautiful thing happened. Each time I would post a *#RoRoLifeNugget* I would get feedback from others who expressed how helpful my nugget had been to them on that day. The private inbox messages were the ones that really touched my heart, as individuals would share how my nugget was an answer to a prayer; the inspiration they needed to make a big decision; or just reassurance that they weren't the only ones going through a hard time.

Since sharing the first *#RoRoLifeNugget* I have made so many new social media friends who approach me while I am out and about to thank me for my nuggets! It is because of all of those people why I was inspired to write this book.

This book is the result of what I have been thinking about, practicing, and sharing over the past year. I have shared personal stories and utilized examples from my friends to teach you how to become a happier you. My mission is to add more happiness to this world by creating tools and techniques that will help you on your journey to lead a happier, more fulfilling life.

As you work through this book over the next 30 days, I believe it will be a reminder that no matter what you are going through, whether the loss of a job, a devastating divorce, or the betrayal of a dear friend, **YOU** are responsible for YOUR happiness.

You have the power to choose *one happy thought* every day, *one happy thought* every hour, or *one happy thought* every minute! The more happy thoughts you choose, I guarantee the result will be a happier you!

Day One

Learn to make happiness enhancing decisions. - Rochelle Gapere

Typically before I make a decision, I ask myself the question, "Will this enhance my happiness?" Usually, sitting with that question causes me to be deliberate about what I am spending my energy on. If you are invited to an event, ask yourself, "Will attending this event enhance my happiness?" If you are asked out on a date, ask yourself, "Will going out with this person, based on what they have demonstrated, enhance my happiness?" Try to get into the practice of questioning yourself about the motive or the return on investment of your time, energy, and effort before you do things. Putting time into thinking about the decisions you make before taking action will help you determine whether you are doing things just for the sake of doing them, or whether it's because society or your family and friends expect you to, or if you truly want to do those things? It causes us to be more conscious of our actions when we pause to explore why we are making certain decisions.

You have to take personal responsibility for your happiness. Until you make your happiness a priority, it will take a backseat to all the other emotions that life can wield at us. This is why I impress upon you to learn what makes you happy. You can't make happiness enhancing decisions if you are unable to identify with clarity the things that make you happy. For instance, I know what it is like to be in a happy and fulfilling relationship because I have been in happy and fulfilling relationships before. I also observe and learn from loved ones who are in happy and fulfilling relationships. When a relationship I was in began to become counter to that, I became uncomfortable. I started comparing what I knew to be a relationship in which I was happy, to the one in which I found myself. Of course, I didn't jump the gun as soon as the relationship hit a rough patch; that would be premature. Instead, I observed the relationship for an allocated period of time, and then acted accordingly. The point is, I knew from personal experience that the relationship in which I found myself was no longer a happy one, and that it had pretty much run its course. I made a happiness enhancing decision by moving on. The initial stages of moving on were not happy, but I knew that my long term happiness depended on making the hard decision to move on so that I could eventually experience a life enhancing relationship again.

For you, it may not be a romantic relationship. It could be a job, or a platonic relationship. What decisions can you make today that could infuse more happiness into your situation? Give it some thought and then start putting it into practice. It doesn't have to be a complete life overhaul, but I can guarantee that once you start with baby steps, you will eventually start asking yourself clarifying questions to ensure that you are

---

10

making decisions that enhance your happiness. What we practice gets stronger, so start practicing!

How will you make your happiness a priority going forward?

Day Two

Are you preparing for what you are wishing or hoping for? – Rochelle Gapere

What I love about this question is that it puts the responsibility to be happy on us. If Mary decides to check running a half marathon off her bucket list in 2018, there are some steps she will have to take to reach her goal. She will probably buy running shoes, commit to a training schedule and also find a running group for training. She literally has to prepare to successfully run the 13.1 miles on race day. If Mary sits at home wishing and hoping to complete the half marathon but fails to prepare, then her goal will evade her. The responsibility for her to complete this goal and happily check this major accomplishment off her bucket list lies with her.

The same method applies for all other happiness life goals. We have to be intentional about our lives and what we want to accomplish. Studies show that setting and accomplishing goals is a sure fire way to increase our happiness. When we have goals to work toward, it gives our lives more meaning. And when we accomplish those goals we feel higher levels of fulfillment. One major goal that I had in my life was to pass the Florida Bar Exam on the first try. I was intentional about fulfilling that goal. To this day, it was the hardest I have ever studied in my life. I was determined to pass that exam on the first try. I diligently studied every day and took practice exams to fulfill my goal. I will never forget how happy I was when I pulled up my results online and saw that I had passed! Over a decade later, I still remember clearly the swell of pride and happiness I felt on that day.

What is a goal that you have set for yourself? It could be a short-term goal or a long-term goal. Either way, you have to be strategic about accomplishing it. Also, you have to be strategic about what is blocking you from fulfilling that goal. Are your priorities centered on the goal? Currently, I have the goal of finishing this book and sending it to edit by a certain date. One of the things that was blocking me from fulling my goal was social media.

I realized I was spending an inordinate amount of time scrolling through my Instagram and Facebook feeds, essentially time I could have been using to fulfill my goal of becoming a published author. As a result, I committed to a social media fast for an entire month. My priorities are now clearly on my goal. I wake up every day and have designated periods of time for writing. By not wasting time on social media, my mind is clearer. I am more focused and am using my time more wisely. Instead of aimlessly scrolling through social media, I am using that time to write. Now, I am in control. The responsibility to write my book falls on me. When I fulfill my dream of becoming an author, it will be another accomplished goal, and it will increase my happiness to know that I am able to make others happy through my writing.

How are you preparing for what you are wishing and hoping for? Things may not be happening according to your timeline, but it is more empowering to start doing things in furtherance of your desires rather than sitting idly by hoping that they will miraculously happen. If you are hoping to be a mother one day, can you offer a close friend who has children to watch her children for a few hours? You get to practice being Mommy for a few hours, and she gets some likely much needed self-care time. If you plan on opening a business someday, can you get started on a business plan, or at minimum, start taking courses that can enhance your skills as an entrepreneur? If you want to be a husband one day, can you find a male mentor who has a successful marriage who would be willing to be your accountability partner as you prepare for that role? As Louis Pasteur said, "Fortune favors the prepared mind!" So start preparing for what you are wishing and hoping for, so that when the time comes you will be ready and equipped to rise to the occasion!

Day Three

Would 8-year-old you be proud of your current life? –Rochelle Gapere

Would 8-year-old you be proud of your current life? Yes? No? Kinda? Sorta? Why? Why not?

Take some time to really ponder the above question. Write it down if you must in your *One Happy Thought at a Time Journal*. I enjoy these types of exercises because it causes me to self-reflect. I think in our current environment we are bombarded by so much external stimulation - Facebook, Twitter, Instagram, Netflix, to name a few - that we don't necessarily spend much time self-reflecting. There is so much power in self-reflection because it forces us to spend quality time examining ourselves from the inside out.

I am asking you about your 8-year-old self because that's typically an age where we are fearless. I asked my friend's 8-year-old daughter, "What do you want to be when you grow up?" And she confidently exclaimed, "A singer, a lawyer, and the President of the United States of America!" Wow! Her bold confidence was impressive and extremely refreshing, I assured her that she could and would do exactly that!

Having that conversation with her is what inspired me to write this *#RoRoLifeNugget*.

It is a sad fact that as we get older we tend to stop dreaming big, bold dreams. Reality sets in and we convince ourselves that our dreams are too farfetched or that they will never happen. We start adjusting our expectations to our level of disappointment and very soon we find ourselves settling into lives that are sometimes uninspiring and unfulfilling. I know this first hand because I found myself in a rut for 2 months in the summer of 2016. For most of my adult life, I remember waking up full of joy and expectation. But for those two months, I was stuck in relationship limbo and I remember waking up thinking more days than not, "This cannot be my life. If this is a preview for the rest of my life, then this is not good!" I knew I had to course correct. A big part of what gave me the courage to move on from that relationship is that I kept asking myself, "Is this the life I envisioned for myself when I was younger? Is this the type of life that happy, fearless, 8-year-old Rochelle looked forward to?" It most certainly was not. So, I eventually moved on.

About 4 months after I moved on from that relationship, I was in Jamaica for the Christmas holidays and my Mom found my yearbooks from St. Andrew Prep, a school I attended between ages 6 through 10, and all my yearbooks throughout high school. In one yearbook in particular, there was a picture of me smiling brightly and underneath the picture was a quote stating, "Dream: to be a lawyer." I remember crying tears of joy and gratitude when I realized I fulfilled my childhood dream. More importantly, when I looked at my innocent face in those books, I knew that little girl would be proud of the woman I had become. She would be proud of some of the tough decisions I made to preserve my happiness. She would be proud that I had the courage to move on from subpar situations. She would be happy that I refused to be stuck, that I chose to create a happy life where I would look forward to waking up filled with joy and expectation every day.

Are you making your 8-year-old self proud? If yes, bravo! I commend you! If no, what steps can you start implementing to course correct? Is there a class you can take? A book you can read? A group you can join for encouragement? What resources do you need to get started? What actionable steps will you take today to reclaim that childlike joy and wonderment? Choose some tasks where you can get easy wins to get your momentum going. Change will not happen overnight, but it will happen if you commit to doing one thing every day to get yourself on the path to happiness.

Day Four

Is it worth giving them your joy?
–Rochelle Gapere

Have you ever been having an amazing day and then you come across someone with a terrible attitude that tries to ruin it for you? Even if the person isn't necessarily upset with you, somehow you get caught in the crossfire of their mood. I have found myself in that situation on a few occasions whether dealing with an impatient customer service representative or a maniac driving crazily down I-95. I remember one example in particular at my old apartment complex. I was having a stellar morning before I went downstairs to the apartment office to pick up a package, only to be met by the office manager who had the nastiest attitude toward me. I knew the attitude was not directed at me because I had not done anything to her. Still, I was really taken aback by her rudeness. While interacting with her I remember thinking, "Is it worth giving her my joy?" In an instance where I could have met her nasty attitude with a nasty attitude myself, I decided to keep quiet, wait for my package, and then kill her with kindness. I got my package and wished her the best day ever with the brightest smile and in the cheeriest voice I could muster. I was so proud of myself and even gave myself an imaginary pat on the back.

See, we cannot control people's actions toward us, but we can control our reaction to them. I don't know what that lady was going through that morning, but I knew I was having a stellar morning and would not allow a 5-minute interaction to steal my joy. Whenever you find yourself in similar situations with people who are intent on being happiness stealers, ask yourself, "Is it worth giving them my joy?"

Recently, my best friend and I made plans to go to a party. It was something we were both looking forward to because we had not been out together in a while. I was disappointed when she called me about 2 hours before we were supposed to meet to tell me that the car wash had lost her car key. When she called she was on her way home to get her spare key and she asked me, "Do you think I should still come? Do you think this is a sign?" She eventually decided to stay home. I told her she had to follow her gut. I was disappointed, but of course I understood her frustration. About 30 minutes later, she called me back excitedly and said, "Girlfriend, let's go! I am not going to let this key thing mess up our plans." I was so happy! The best part is while we were having fun at the party, the guy from the car wash text messaged her to tell her that he had found her car key. We were so happy and relieved! The good news added an extra element of fun to the party. She didn't allow a situation that had a clear solution to steal her joy. Yes, she was rightfully frustrated that the key was lost, but the car wash guy had reassured her that they would pay to replace it. And fortunately she had a spare key. When we are faced with hiccups in our plans or have to interact with rude people, we sometimes have the tendency to get upset, wallow in self-pity, or mope around and complain to anyone willing to listen. However, ask yourself, "Is it worth giving this situation or this person my joy?" Was it worth it to me to give the attitudinal office lady my joy? No! Was it worth it to my best friend to give the car wash guy, who clearly made a mistake, her joy? No! Is it worth it to you to give your nosey neighbor, your temperamental boss, the rude customer service agent your joy? In the grand scheme of things, I can bet not!

It is pretty simple math, the less joy we have in our lives, the less happy we will be. The more joy we have in our lives, the happier we will be. So protect your joy and protect it fiercely!

Day Five

Do something today that makes your heart overflow with happiness! – *Rochelle Gapere*

When was the last time you did something that made your heart overflow with happiness? How often do you engage in activities that make your heart overflow with happiness? The more often you do what makes your heart happy, the happier you will be. I think we can all agree on that last statement. So why then, do we put off our happiness for a future time?

A friend of mine was going through a rough period. Usually, she is very joyous despite what's going on in her life. She has a similar optimistic outlook like I do. So I was pretty concerned when she could not seem to shake her funk after a couple weeks. I could tell she was not her usual self. One day, while we were chatting, I asked her, "When was the last time you went to the beach to watch the sunrise?" She paused for a second and then replied, "It has been such a long time that I cannot remember." I was pretty stunned and I said to her, "But that is one of your favorite things to do. You love that! You even had a sunrise beach wedding!" I suggested that she start making sunrise watching at the beach a priority again. She agreed. A few days later she happily told me that she had gone to the beach to watch the sunrise and reported how much it lifted her mood.

We know the things that make us happy, but we neglect doing them. I understand that life sometimes gets in the way. However, it is up to us to make our happiness a priority. One thing I know that guarantees my happiness is a day at the beach or at the pool. I love bodies of water. In summer 2017, I promised myself that my summer hobby would be pool or beach lounging. I even started a hashtag #summerhobby2017 where I would take a picture to document my day at the pool or beach. I looked forward to honoring the promise to myself by carving out one day, sometimes 2 days every weekend to spend a couple of hours at the pool or beach. The beautiful thing is that because I shared it on social media I had friends who joined in on the fun too.

Before making the commitment to my summer hobby, I had stopped going to the pool or the beach regularly even though I knew it was one of the things that guaranteed me pure happiness. How had that happened? I allowed life to get in the way. But, I am pleased that I recommitted to my pool and beach days, because now I look back on summer 2017 as one filled with such great joy and wonderful memories. Now, I consciously focus on the things that make me happy and make a concerted effort to do them regularly. The more I engage in the activities that make me happy, the happier life becomes. Take time to write out a list of the things that you know guarantee your happiness, whether it is a phone call with your mom every week, reading a fictional book every month, going for a massage, dancing to your favorite song, or going for a morning hike or walk, and make it a priority to do it often. It doesn't have to be a big production like a two-week international vacation. No, start with simple small joys and very soon you will see that your day-to-day life will be infused with more happiness. As Maya Angelou rightfully and profoundly stated in one of my all-time favorite quotes, "Love life, engage in it, give it all you've got. Love it with passion, because life truly does give back, many times over, what you put into it."

Day Six

Be grateful for your portion in life!
– Rochelle Gapere

No matter what situation you find yourself in today, be grateful for your portion. You only have to watch five minutes of the morning news, as the reporters discuss all the doom and gloom in this world, for you to realize that your situation could always be worse. I know this may not sound like a "happy thought," but it is a way to shift your thinking and put your life in perspective. The mere fact that you are reading this book right now means that you are alive and that you have vision. Your eyes are healthy and functioning and your brain is capable of making sense of these words. Not only did you wake up, but more than likely you woke up with a roof over your head, which means you are not homeless.

In fact, it was a homeless woman who affirmed my thinking on gratitude. You could say I have an affinity for those who live on the streets. Each time I see a homeless person I try to be kind to them. I also think about what circumstances caused their homelessness. Did they lose a job? Are they mentally ill? Where are their family members and friends? About 10 years ago, I befriended a homeless lady named Blossom, who I now lovingly refer to as my "adopted mom." Although I rarely see her these days, Blossom helps me keep things in perspective. Her life took a tragic turn when she had an accident that claimed the lives of her children one night after drinking at a party. Since that incident, she lost her marriage and her home, and her life pretty much turned upside down. Unfortunately, she ended up on the street. Blossom's life is a reminder that in a split second everything can change. One night of partying and having one too many drinks ended in a tragedy. Yet, anytime I run into Blossom in Downtown Miami, she always greets me with so much love. It isn't her ideal situation, but she still expresses gratitude for her portion in life- mainly her life-because she knows she could have died that night too. Unfortunately, I have run into many like Blossom on the streets of Miami.

The garage where I park my car is across the street from a building where many homeless people find shelter. Each time I walk pass them it puts my life in perspective. There are times when I am walking into my office building where I do not want to be bothered with having to work that day. However, I look around my surroundings and breathe a sigh of gratitude that I woke up in a comfortable bed with a roof over my head and I have a job to go to. It is easy to lose sight of what we are lacking in a world where we are constantly encouraged to buy more, want more, or do more. But there is so much power and peace of mind in focusing on what you currently have. The minute you start giving thanks for what you have, you will recognize that you have way more than you even realized. Remember, life could possibly be better,

---

but it also could be worse. So be grateful for your portion while you have it. This is the only day like this you will ever have in your life. Once today passes you will never get it back!

Day Seven

Grateful that God woke me up this morning. He didn't have to but He did. And for that, I am beyond thankful. –Rochelle Gapere

I wrote this quote after waking up to two separate Facebook posts that a friend from my old neighborhood in Jamaica, as well as a friend of mine's Mother had passed away. I was pretty shocked about the childhood friend because he was no older than 40. He had so much life ahead of him. My friend's Mom wasn't older than 65, but had been fighting an illness for quite some time. The knowledge of both deaths on the same day made my heart heavy. It also made me extremely grateful that I woke up that morning. Not only did I wake up, but all the people closest to me woke up that morning too.

I am not sure about you, but there are times that I take waking up for granted. In other words, I assume that it is a given that I must wake up. Waking up is a privilege not a right, and for me, knowing what a privilege it is to wake up makes me live each day more fully. To be honest, tomorrow isn't promised for any of us, so while we have today we may as well make the most of it. Having that outlook has caused me to shake worry and angst quickly. When I find myself in a state of worry about something or even a bit sad because something is not going like I hope and is beyond my control, I ask myself, "If this were your last day on earth, would you want to spend it being sad or worried?" Usually that question allows me to refocus on the blessing of being alive rather than whatever is not going my way. As my favorite pastor, Bishop Joseph Walker III says, "Once you have pulse, you have possibility," which is another way of saying, "Once you have life, you have hope." And it is true! If you are alive you can change your circumstances. The only thing permanent is death. The mere fact that I woke up this morning means that I can change anything within my power that I do not like. Also, because I know that tomorrow is not promised to me, I try to do everything in my power to enjoy the present moment because that is the only moment I am certain that I have.

If today were your last day on earth, how would you like to spend it? If you live your life with that question in mind, you will come to realize that certain arguments aren't worth having and you'll stop wasting your energy on people who don't deserve it. You will make the effort to treasure every waking moment and fill it with what makes you happy, and you will also be in a state of gratitude knowing that life is a gift that you are privileged to have. Everything may not be exactly as you hoped or imagined, but you have life so you have the opportunity to change your thinking and your habits.

I hope after reading this you will challenge yourself,

especially in tough times, to focus on the big picture - that you are blessed with life, which is no guarantee. Appreciate each day that you!

Day Eight

Maybe it's not working out the way you think it should because God wants to exceed your expectations. –Rochelle Gapere

How many times has a door been slammed shut and you keep knocking on it over and over again? How many times have you seen a red flag in a relationship, but you kept pressing along hoping that things would change or get better? There have been instances where relationships were not working out in my favor and I chose to keep pouring more of my energy into situations that clearly had passed their expiration dates. It was not until God slammed certain doors shut in my life that I got the point and moved on. And sometimes I moved on pouting, yet had no choice but to move on. Inevitably, time would pass and I would see exactly why the door was slammed shut, and realized that God closed the door to steer me in a better or more rewarding direction.

Recently, I attended a close friend's wedding and while I was sitting there, I had an "aha moment," and realized her past relationships did not work out because God wanted to exceed her expectations and her husband's treatment and adoration of her far exceeded any man she had dated prior. We have been close friends for many years, so I was there through the ebbs and flows of her romantic life. I saw when she faced massive disappointment when her then boyfriend indirectly forced her to break up with him. Imagine if she had stayed in that relationship trying to force him to finally marry and do right by her. She would have missed the blessing of her amazing God-ordained husband. To be honest, her husband was a better partner for her in every sense of the word than her ex. Her wedding was a perfect reminder, and physical evidence, that when we wait on God to do His thing, He will exceed our expectations.

Maybe for you, it's not a relationship. Maybe it's the job you did not get after you made it to the final interview. Maybe it is the school you didn't get accepted into even though your application was incredible. Trust that there is something better awaiting you. You may not be able to see it clearly in the moment, but as time passes you will be able to look back and realize that the thing that did not work out was a huge blessing because it led you to a job, relationship, school, and/or experience that exceeds your expectations.

Day Nine

You honor yourself when you treat yourself well. And you should. –Rochelle Gapere

How are you treating YOUR self? Pause. Take a moment and observe yourself as if you were a stranger watching yourself from the outside. Would that stranger think, "Wow _____ (insert your name here) treats himself or herself very well?" Or would they be appalled? If you are totally honest with yourself while completing this exercise, you will either be dismayed or you will feel proud and empowered.

I have done this exercise numerous times in my life. For the most part, I have been pretty happy with what I have observed, but there have been times where I was shocked and dismayed. Some of those times I observed myself allowing people to take advantage of me, disrespect me, or be unkind to me. And yes, allowing people to mistreat you is a form of you not treating yourself well.

I know you have heard the phrase, "You teach people how to treat you." A person knows how to treat you based on how they observe you treating yourself or by how you allow them to treat you. I treat myself well by carving out time every single day to have "me time." This "me time" may take on different forms and some days consist of more "me time" than others. But for the most part, I make sure that every day I do something special just for me. For example, I set aside at least 30 minutes where I sit in complete and utter silence to be one with my thoughts. I don't check my phone or email. I don't listen to music. I literally sit or drive in silence and "get my mind right." I also treat myself well by eating a balanced diet, exercising, praying, reading books that edify me, and consciously doing things to better myself. When I observe myself these days, I am proud of how I treat Rochelle. I make Rochelle a priority. I fill her tank with happy thoughts and positive experiences. I shield her from negativity as best as I can. And I make choices that are in her best interest 99% of the time. I have one self, and while I have her I will choose to honor her.

I hope you too will start honoring yourself by carving out time for yourself and create experiences that honor you. After all, you cannot pour from an empty tank. You know how you like to be treated, so fill yourself up with goodness as much as you can and as best as you can.

Day Ten

Focus on your blessings more than your problems! – **Rochelle Gapere**

It is so easy to get fixated on all the things that are going wrong that we sometimes overlook ALL the things that are going right. The mere fact that you woke up this morning in your right mind, with your heart beating, and air to breathe is something to be thankful for and get excited about!

Far too often, we get sidetracked by our problems and miss the opportunity to focus on our blessings. What you focus on expands and multiplies. How many times have you thought about something and then all of a sudden you keep seeing that thing? For example, if you think about buying a certain car, soon afterward you start seeing that car everywhere. So why is it so hard for most of us to get this simple concept? Our minds are so trained to think and talk about our problems that breaking that habit becomes tough. If we want love, abundance, and happiness, why not focus on love, abundance, and happiness?

My gratitude practice helps me significantly with focusing on my blessings. Each morning when I wake up, I immediately think about three things I am grateful for. I challenge myself to express gratitude for three *new/different* things every day. It could be as simple as "I am grateful for comfortable pillows to sleep on." Or more important things such as, "I am grateful for my healthy kidneys." Having to find three new things each day makes the process a fun and exciting challenge! Some days I even tweet them to get my followers in on the fun. My gratitude practice sets the tone for my day. Before my mind can wander off into wherever it feels like wandering off to, I capture my thoughts with gratitude and good energy. And voila, I control how I start my day rather than my day controlling me! As I am writing this chapter I will share the three things that I am grateful for today:

1) I am grateful for the opportunity to write my first book;

2) I am grateful for my mother who nurtured my love for reading and writing by taking me to Tom Redcam Library in Kingston, Jamaica when I was a child; and

3) I am grateful for healthy fingers that can type on a keyboard.

Train your mind to focus on more of what you want. What are the three things you are grateful for today? Make a habit of writing the three things you are grateful for every day in your *One Happy Thought at a Time Journal*!

Day Eleven

Stress is a choice. So is peace. – Unknown

What are YOU choosing? Peace of mind is PRICE-LESS! The best part is that the choice is yours. And let me be clear, things don't have to be "perfect" for one to have peace. You can choose to have peace in the midst of a storm. Ask yourself, "What is this situation or circumstance here to teach me?" Then choose all the paths that lead you towards peace. In other words, grow through what you go through. Read new books. Pray. Journal. Exercise. Take a new class on a subject that interests you. Go on new adventures.

Spend your energy on things that make you better, rather than sitting back and stressing yourself out. You will be surprised to see how soon your energy shifts when you use your time on what edifies you rather than things that detract from your peace of mind. Never forget that you have the power to cut out stressors and energy stealers! If talking to a particular person stresses you out, stop answering your phone.

If it is someone you must communicate with, then choose the medium that causes the least stress. Send them a text message or an email rather than talking to them and hearing their voice. Controlling the medium of communication also gives you the power to control how much of your time you will allow them to have access to.

If you know that certain people destabilize your peace, then do not go to places where you know you'll see them! These things seem pretty straightforward, but you would be surprised to know how often people do things against their best interest and contrary to their peace.

I know that watching the news robs me of my peace. Instead, I have allotted a certain amount of time each day, usually in the afternoons after lunch, to read the news. I realized that watching or reading the news early in the morning and absorbing all the negativity was robbing me of my peace, so I changed that behavior. I also no longer attend events that will rob me of my happiness or peace. I will send a gift rather than go to places that will pollute my energy or peace of mind. When I get an invite to attend an event, I ask myself, "Will I be better having attended this event?"

If yes, I will make an effort to attend. If no, I stay at home and do things that I know will keep me in a peaceful state or bring me joy, such as reading.

I have made a conscious effort to fiercely protect my peace and I have been happier because of it.

Today, start your practice of choosing peace. And if you already exist in a peaceful state, don't allow anyone to destabilize it.

Stress is a choice and so is peace!

Day Twelve

***Don't get sidetracked by negativity and miss the great things God is about to do in your life.** -Rochelle Gapere*

Choose to reduce and/or eliminate the time you spend with people who are committed to being negative. Instead, choose to be around people who are optimistic, positive, faithful and hopeful! It is amazing how often people allow themselves to be around people who are negative Nancys and have terrible attitudes. You have the power to choose what you respond to. You don't have to answer the phone. You don't have to reply to a text message or email. You don't have to go to environments with negative people or negative energy. Barring work, because I am pretty sure you have to go there...for now! However, you can, at least, limit your time around your coworker(s) with negative attitudes as much as possible.

Be extremely protective and cognizant of who and what you allow in your space. Energy is contagious! As Oprah put it, "Surround yourself with only people who are going to lift you higher." Today (and for the rest of your life, really! LOL!) avoid negative people, negative environments, and negativity overall like the plague. You have ONE precious life and while you are blessed to have it, make a conscious effort to spend it with people, or on things that enhance your life, bring you peace and happiness, and make you better. Don't block your blessings entertaining anything that isn't God's absolute BEST for your life.

Day Thirteen

Perspective: Have you ever had a bad day?

While enjoying a pool day with some friends one afternoon a friend of mine asked me, "Have you ever had a bad day?" I thought for a few seconds and then replied, "I have had bad moments. I have never allowed those moments to last for a day!" Then I added, "Of course, I have had bad things happen to me, but I believe my perspective is what differs from most." He said my perspective was unique and refreshing. My Mom dislikes when I say this, but I always say, "If tomorrow were my last day on earth, how would I live today?" As a result, I make the MOST of my 'today' every single day. This is especially helpful on the days when things aren't going my way. I ask myself, "If I were to die tomorrow do I want to spend today irritated, annoyed, upset, or sad?" And then, I snap out of it!!

If asking the right questions doesn't work, I'll use a different strategy. For example, I'll give myself an allotted time to wallow in sadness or self-pity. I might say, "It's now 9:30 a.m., I am going to give myself two hours to be sad about this situation and then I am going to move on." I make a conscious deliberate decision two hours later to do something I am certain is guaranteed to give me joy, whether it is dancing to my favorite song or reading inspirational quotes to lift my mood.

The beauty of this is that I am choosing simple accessible tools to lift my mood. I don't have to plan anything elaborate or future-based to reclaim my joy. I can change my mind and reclaim it in the moment. I use my phone to play my favorite songs or I google positive quotes and then read a few. In that moment my spirit shifts.

Life is too short and too fragile to be consumed with what is beyond my control. So much of what worries us are self-created issues. Living in the future or being obsessed with the past are two ways in which we cause ourselves unnecessary worry. For one, we can't change our past. We can learn the lessons and move forward by consciously choosing not to repeat the same mistakes.

I know, I know – everyone thinks about their past at some point. But we can be reflective on the past, without getting stuck there. Although there are a few things in my past that I would certainly do differently, I know different choices would have produced different outcomes that I am not sure I would be fully satisfied with either. One of my favorite bible verses is Romans 8:28: "All things work together for good for those who love God and are called according to his purpose." My interpretation is that every single occurrence whether good or bad is working together for my good. We hear a similar sentiment in the common saying, "Everything happens for a reason." If I were to change one thing in my past, I wouldn't be where I am today. And that's what happiness is, accepting where you are right now. Besides, it's impossible to change the past, so why focus your energy on it?

As for the future, reasonable planning is necessary, but overthinking, ruminating, or becoming anxious about it (especially as it concerns other people in your future) proves frustrating and futile. We can't control people. People control themselves. And we can only control our own behavior.

Bad moments are inevitable. They are a part of the human experience. Without the rain, we wouldn't appreciate the sunny days. Without sad times, we wouldn't appreciate the happy ones as much. Knowing that bad moments are building blocks to a positive outcome is what keeps me going. Today, spend time reflecting on the lessons you have learned from bad moments.

Perhaps you learned to make better, more informed decisions. Have faith that your bad moments will pass, and while you have your bad moments, look for the silver lining. A bad thing may have happened to you, but you are still blessed with life and able to experience something more. You still have oxygen to breathe. You still have eyes to read these words. You still have hands to hold this book. Perspective is everything. Change your perspective and you will change your life.

Day Fourteen

Stop imagining the worst case scenario and use that energy to imagine the BEST case scenario.
— Rochelle Gapere

They both take the same amount of energy, so why not focus on the good stuff?

I wake up in the morning and think, "What's the BEST that could happen today?" And you know what? Lots of great things tend to happen to me, and for me, daily! I am not saying it is easy, but I consciously refresh my mind every morning with positive thinking. There is a scripture that says, "Do not conform to the pattern of this world, but be transformed by the renewing of your mind" (Romans 12:2). The renewing of my mind focuses on goodness. I fill my mind with goodness by reading God's word, praying, meditating, declaring affirmations, and even singing.

I want you to pause for a moment and think about all the bullet points on your to-do list today. You can make a mental note of your list, or you can write it down in your *One Happy Thought at a Time Journal*. Now review the list, and for each item that you have identified, think about the BEST possible scenario that could happen in each particular instance. Perhaps you have a presentation at school or work. Assuming you have prepared as best as you can, start thinking of the best-case scenario for your presentation. Rather than think, "I am going to mess up the presentation today" think about all the best possible outcomes. "I will do well on my presentation...I will be an effective communicator...and the audience will understand my message and receive it positively." You see where I am going with this? Your mood and energy probably shifted positively by doing this exercise. Also, by doing so, you are now probably feeling more confident about the presentation. You can apply this exercise in many different ways. Try to use this approach each time you find yourself worrying about a possible outcome. Use your energy to focus on the best possible outcome and you will find that the best possible outcome happens more often than not.

What are you expecting today?

Day Fifteen

Do not allow fear to hold you hostage. One brave decision can change your entire life for the better. – Rochelle Gapere

Fear will stop you from participating fully in life! Acknowledge the fear and be honest about it, but don't let it handicap you from making decisions that can enhance your life for the better. How many times have you allowed fear to hold you hostage? Fear of failure. Fear of rejection. Fear of death. Fear of losing. One of the bravest decisions I have ever made was walking away from a long-term relationship when I was 35 years old. I remember fear trying to set in when I made up my mind to move on. Fearful thoughts such as, "Suppose I don't find someone better?" and "Will I ever get married and have children?" would surface every now and then. The fears were unfounded.

After walking away from that relationship, I didn't get married or have children right away. However, that one brave decision opened up a world of opportunity for me. Pain put me on the path to purpose and sparked creativity within me. I would not have written this book you are holding had I not taken the brave step to move on. It was through moving on that I realized I needed to share my perspective on deliberately choosing happiness despite life's monkey wrenches. I launched my happiness consultancy business as a result of that storm. I had the courage to take a six and a half week sabbatical, which I dubbed *#RObattical*, where I traveled to four different countries, numerous cities, and met many wonderful people. I would not have had that experience, or made those connections had I not taken the leap. That one brave decision has paid so many dividends, and I know I have only touched the iceberg on the immense goodness that is impending in my life.

What is the one thing that deep in your gut you know you should do, but have allowed fear to block you from taking that leap? An exercise that works for me, and I am sure will work for you too, is to make a pros and cons list. What are the benefits of overcoming the fear and what are the cons of succumbing to the fear? Seeing your list in your own handwriting will make the right choices evident and clear.

For me, when I made my pros and cons list about whether to move on, it looked something like this – Pros: 1. meet, fall in love, and then marry my soulmate; 2. have a happy and stable family life to raise my children, where our relationship would be a true example of love; 3. be in a happy, loving, and healthy relationship with a man who adores and cherishes me; or Cons: 1. stay in a relationship that I know wasn't God's best; 2. always wonder if I'd settled; 3. be moderately happy. This is just a short example of some of my entries. After writing my list, it was glaringly clear that I needed to end the relationship, and the hope of a better future gave me the courage to move on. I also knew that with or without a partner, I would be better off on my own, where I knew I would continue to create, and live a happy and fulfilled life.

If there is something that you desire or want to do, do it! Do not let fear hold you hostage. Just ask yourself this one question: "If I fail, what's the worst that can happen." If your answer is not death, complete financial ruin for the rest of your life, or a significant illness...do it! There is nothing to fear. Worst case scenario, you fail and learn. Failure is just another opportunity for you to grow and improve. The best thing that can happen is that you live a life beyond your wildest imagination! That is worth your bravery! Remember we're focusing on the best case scenarios these days! What's the BEST that could happen if you released your fear today? Be brave!

Day Sixteen

Protect yourself from emotionally draining interactions by putting buffers in place to preserve your happiness! –Rochelle Gapere

Have you ever been having a good day and then you interact with someone and when the interaction is over you feel your mood changes in a negative rather than positive way? I have a friend who I love dearly, but anytime I talk to her on the phone I am left feeling emotionally depleted because she always has a constant barrage of complaints. It would be easy to just say stop being her friend, but beyond her negative view on life, she is kind, caring, and she has been loyal throughout the course of our friendship. I treasure her. You may have people in your life who you love, but you know when you engage with them they too deplete your energy.

Self-preservation means protecting oneself from harmful people or things. Protecting yourself from negative people is necessary to protecting your happiness and peace of mind. I believe there is a way to interact with people, whom you love, but who also have the tendency to be potentially draining without cutting them off. For instance, when dealing with my friend, I know there are times of the day when it is better to communicate with her.

I rarely ever speak to her in the morning, because I like to set the tone of my mornings with positivity. I minimize how often I speak to her, and when I do it's at the end of my work day in the evening. Doing so allows me to engage with her fully, but also I know that when we end our interaction, I can then do something that is guaranteed to lift my mood, such as listen to music, read a blog about positivity, or watch a television show that recalibrates my mood.

Everyone isn't wired to be positive naturally and some people have to actively make a conscious effort to cut negative thinking out of their lives. In fact, I can see firsthand how my friend has evolved over our friendship because of her interactions with me. It makes me proud to see her grow. She has also helped me grow in the sense that I have more patience for people's differences.

However, I also know that I won't allow her negative mindset to affect my mood, so I do everything in my power to protect it. In a perfect world, interactions with people would always leave you feeling warm and fuzzy inside. However, we don't live in a perfect world world, so we have to adjust our interactions according-ly. In the wise words of Hans F. Hansen, "People insp-ire you, or they drain you – pick them wisely."

Day Seventeen

Imagine your life 15 years from now! Are you living your life right now in alignment with how you imagine yourself?
– Rochelle Gapere

For the past couple months, I have been taking various courses on happiness, personal development, and well-being. In one particular class, *Leading the Life You Want*, my professor asked the class to time travel 15 years from now and consider all the parts of our lives. He then posed the following questions- "Imagine your future." "Why are you doing what you are doing?" "What impact are you having?" "What are others saying about you?"

I will be honest the first thing that sent a lightning bolt through my head is that 15 years from now I will be 51 years old!! I can't tell when, if ever, I really sat down and imagined a 51-year-old Rochelle. It was a wake-up call for me! At 51 years old, I would have lived more than half of my life! I want to use my life to create a powerful legacy and to make a positive contribution to the world.

Yet, up to this point in my life, I haven't taken intentional actions that will create the type of legacy that I want. This exercise was timely.

Right now, I want you to put this book down for a moment and take 15 minutes to imagine your future 15 years from now. How old will you be? Where do you imagine yourself living? What impact will you be having in the world, in your community, and in your family? How are you earning money? How are you taking care of yourself mentally, emotionally, physically, and spiritually?

How do you modify your current circumstance in an effective way so that you are able to align your present with the future you have imagined for yourself?

This exercise was beyond powerful for me. On a personal level, I imagine that 15 years from now I will be happily married to an amazing partner and the mother of two healthy children. I imagine that I will be a healthy, happy woman who exercises at least 4 times a week, eats a well-balanced diet, and takes time for self-care. After articulating what I desired my future to look like, I then paused to see if my current life was leading me in that direction. For starters, I can't predict when or if I will get married. However, what I have the power to do presently is to be mindful and purposeful about the type of men I date.

I am only interested in dating marriage minded men who have integrity and who demonstrate through their words and actions that they are committed to being good husbands.

As for being a mom, I have been very diligent about

—

eating healthily, exercising regularly and taking the necessary vitamins, so that if or when the time comes for me to venture into motherhood, I will be as healthy as possible within my power to carry healthy babies. If I plan to be a woman who exercises 4 times a week at 51, then I need to form those healthy exercise habits right now. Do you see where I am going with this? In order for me to live the life I imagine at 51, I have to practice and start implementing healthy habits now at the age of 36.

Of course, there are many things outside of our control. None of us know if we will live to see the next 15 years or where life will take us. However, if we live each day with clarity about what we want our lives to look like whether 5 hours, 5 days, 5 years or 15 years from now, it will empower us to live purposeful lives. There is power in purposeful living. And the power is yours!

Whether you took a mental note or you actually jotted down on paper what you imagine your life to be 15 years from now, starting today I implore you to make bold steps in that direction. If you are doing things currently that are opposite to your desires, don't get down on yourself or be discouraged. Knowledge is power! Now that you know better, you have the power to do better. So, make your action plan to march confidently towards the "happy you, 15 years in the future!"

Day Eighteen

Be kind to yourself! Everyone makes mistakes! –
Rochelle Gapere

I was babysitting my godchildren one weekend and at about 5 a.m. one morning my goddaughter rushed into my room in tears. My immediate thought was that she had a bad dream. After getting her to calm down, I asked her what was wrong. She timidly stated that she accidentally wet her bed. In her dream she thought she went to the bathroom, but she really didn't and now her bed was wet. I looked at her and said, "Ok. So you made a mistake. Mistakes are ok. We aren't perfect. There is no need to be so hard on yourself about something we can fix." I could see the relief on her little face. It hurt me that she felt that she had to be so hard on herself for an innocent mistake. I realized that this was a teachable moment and so I asked her, "If your baby brother told you that he wet the bed, what would you say to him?" She replied, "I would tell him that everything is ok and not to cry." I said, "Well, treat yourself with the same kind of kindness you would treat your baby brother." I could see the lightbulb go off in her mind. I hoped it would be a lesson she would hold onto for life.

This is an example of having compassion with one's self. Self-compassion is defined as offering the same kindness to ourselves that we would give to a friend. Rather than beat ourselves up with judgment and shame when we make mistakes, we should treat ourselves with kindness and love. We all make mistakes. None of us is perfect. Our imperfections are a part of being human. The sooner we are able to work through a hardship, the happier we will become. Think about it, if my goddaughter spent the rest of her day beating herself up about wetting her bed, she would have had a bad day at school, which could possibly have led to her having a bad mood at her after-school activities. It was important to me for her to exercise self-compassion because I knew once she realized that it was a mistake, and that mistakes happen, then she could get on happily with her day. And she did.

It is easy to get stuck on our regrets and our mistakes with thoughts such as, "I should have done that better or why didn't I do it that way or how could I let myself down." However, once we accept that mistakes are part of the human experience and that we cannot change our past, then we can move forward into a happier future. We are not our mistakes. Self-compassion allows us to own our mistakes, but to also lovingly look at the lessons.

I make it a practice to be kind to myself. I speak to myself as lovingly as I would speak to a best friend going through a similar situation: "Rochelle, you made those decisions on the knowledge you had then. You can't use your new level of enlightenment to judge a situation that happened two years ago. You did your best." I can't tell you how helpful being compassionate with myself has been, especially in situations where I think I should have known better. Forgiving myself for past mistakes and being kind to myself has added to my happiness in more profound ways than I would have imagined. I realize that doing a bad thing doesn't make me a bad person. I realize that not accomplishing one goal doesn't diminish the hundreds of goals I have accomplished. I have given myself room to own my mistake, learn from it, grow and become better. I implore you today to be kind to yourself. Stop replaying the reels of shoulda, coulda, wouldas in your life. You have your present and you have your future. Don't allow your past to damage them. Be kind to yourself and confidently move in the direction of what brings you joy.

Day Nineteen

There is supreme power in deliberately tailoring the messaging that infiltrates your thoughts on a daily basis! What can your mind use less of? Try doing away with it and replacing those thoughts with better ones! -
Rochelle Gapere

On November 30, 2017 I decided to go on a social media fast for the month of December. It wasn't a hard decision to make. The year was coming to a close and I realized there were some goals that I still needed to accomplish for 2017, so I needed to limit all distractions. I am not sure about you, but if I total up the amount of time I spend scrolling through my Instagram and Facebook feeds in a single day, it would be about 2 hours total combined. I decided that I not only wanted, but needed, to redirect my energy into more productive pursuits.

As I am writing this book, I am sitting in Nashville, Tennessee for the Christmas holiday before the fireplace and I just finished reading a very good book. As I wondered what I could do next to occupy my time, I decided to write this entry. Usually, I would have picked up my phone and spent at minimum thirty minutes on social media. Now, without that distraction, I can use my time more effectively. Voila, this entry!

Over the past few weeks that I have been on my fast, I have enjoyed more meaningful conversations with friends that I typically wouldn't have because we rely on our social media as a sufficient source of contact. Friends, who have not seen me on their feeds, reach out to me directly on text message or phone calls, and we have colorful in-depth conversations. These conversations have been extremely fulfilling and have added to my joy in more ways than I can count. I almost forgot the art of having real time phone conversations.

Another benefit of my social media fast is that I actively seek the information or entertainment I want. On any given day on my social media feed, it is filled with posts ranging from doom and gloom to happiness and triumph. The doom and gloom posts weigh heavily on my spirit in the moment as I scroll past it, and sometimes even longer depending on the news story. Now, I control when and how much time I want to allot to the news. Of course, I enjoy the happy posts- the marriage proposals, the baby announcements, and the promotions.

But I also realize that my friends now message me directly to tell me the latest updates on their lives so I am able to celebrate with them in a more substantive way than just a like or a quick comment on their Facebook feed.

This change has allowed me to become more present in my life. While Uber-ing around Miami, I actually look out the window and pay attention to the landscape. Now, I have a new appreciation for the things I would miss or take for granted because my head would be looking down at my phone scrolling through social media. The beautiful thing about my social media fast is that I am fully engaged with family and friends in social settings. They have my undivided attention. It's a pleasant surprise; because initially when I decided to do the fast, I thought I would miss social media. However, I am now on day 29 and I am happier without it than I am with it. I have reconnected with myself in a deeper way, found so many new interesting things to occupy my time and have now deliberately tailored the messaging that can infiltrate my thoughts on a daily basis.

Social media of course, has many benefits, but going forward, I am going to use it in a more structured way-one that continues to enhance my happiness rather than stifles it. I hope you will give a social media detox a try. It may not be for a month like I did, but I think a few days or a couple of hours in exchange for new activities that add to your happiness is worth a try!

Day Twenty

Let go off littleness and strive for limitless.
-Rochelle Gapere

One of the greatest disservices we do to ourselves is to sell ourselves short. We tend to think in terms of lack instead of abundance. We limit ourselves in terms of what we can achieve and what we can accomplish. We look at others and think why them, why not me? Rather than if he or she can do it, so can I! We should strive for our ultimate best. There are times, of course, where we feel stagnant in life. However, that is when we need to get outside of our comfort zones by visiting new places, reading new books, or doing other activities to challenge our way of thinking.

Whenever I feel myself getting stagnant, I like to go to the beach and observe the water. There is something about the vast ocean that reinvigorates me. The vastness of the ocean is symbolic to me as it represents the limitless opportunities available to me. I have the power to tap into them, like I have the ability to go into the ocean.

I also make it a habit to read *Success Magazine* which

is where I get inspiration from others who have pushed beyond limits and obstacles to live successful lives. As the popular adage goes, "Success leaves clues." I do not believe God placed me or you on this earth to live mediocre lives. We are here to live life more abundantly.

It is unfortunate that as a society we have been conditioned to think in terms of lack, competition, and finite resources. The scarcity mindset leads one to experience a life not fully lived. An individual with an abundant mindset lives a full life overflowing with happiness, knowing that resources are infinite. Someone with an abundant mentality is an optimist and is genuinely happy for others when they achieve success. Conversely, those with a scarcity mindset are competitive and resent other's success. There are more than enough resources on this earth for all of us to enjoy and share. We just have to let go of little and think limitless. Limitless is defined as "without end, limit or boundaries." How can you take the limits off your thoughts today?

Once you change your mind, you can change your life. If you believe there is more than enough money, happiness, and goodness to go around in this world, then you will be able to celebrate when others have and experience those things. Abundance is our birthright. You deserve an abundance of love, an abundance of peace, an abundance of health, and an abundance of prosperity. As the famous quote suggests: "The secret to having it all is believing you already do."

Day Twenty-One

God is not a one hit wonder. If He did it before, He can certainly do it again.
–Rochelle Gapere

Think about all the times God came through for you in a crunch! If He did it before, why do you doubt that He is able to do it again? I want you to try an exercise that I enjoy doing and do pretty often when I need to bolster my faith. Look back at some of your most brilliant successes, stunning comebacks, amazing catches, and winning ideas. Now make a note of them. I am certain before some of those things manifested in your life you were probably wrought with fear or anxiety. However, eventually it all worked out, right? Hopefully, by doing this exercise it will help you to have a faith booster. God worked things out for you that time, so what stops Him from working things out for you this time? Absolutely nothing! You just have to strengthen your faith.

One of the many reasons I keep a prayer journal is to remind myself of God's goodness in my life. I have been journaling since I was 17 years old, which means

I have approximately 20 years of journals that contain hundreds and hundreds of answered prayers. If I ever dare forget God's goodness in my life, I pull out an old journal from a period of my life where my faith wavered, but where God came through. Whether it was sending an angel to help me when my luggage was lost en route to Morocco, or helping me to land my current job even though I was not searching for a job at the time, or the thousands of other prayers I have prayed, He has always had my back. And to be clear, there were times when I didn't get what I initially desired, but He came through bigger and better each time.

It is also why I celebrate others' wins, because if God can do it for them, then certainly He can do it for me! I have two very close friends who were blessed with their *dream* guys and ideal partners at the ages of 38 and 40! I happily and excitedly celebrate every engagement, engagement photo, marriage, baby shower, and anniversary, because…guess what? The same God who did it for them can absolutely do it for me too! It is important to have faith and a positive attitude when you are in a season of expectation.

A song that I love, and one that I play to encourage myself when I need a reminder of God's faithfulness is Tye Tribett's, If He Did It Before (Same God). I love this part in particular:

> *Please be, encouraged, this is not the first storm you've been through*
> *You've been through worse; you didn't come this far just to lose*

He knows your needs so take no thoughts on
what you lost
God will restore, and this is how I'm sure
If He did it before, He can do it again
Same God right now, same God back then
If He did it before, He can do it again
Same God right now, same God back then.

If God did it before, don't you think He can do it again... and again... and again... ad infinitum?

Day Twenty—Two

While you have life: live it fully, tell & show your loved ones how much you love them, and deflect all bad vibes. –Rochelle Gapere

One morning while I was scrolling through Instagram, I saw a meme that deeply resonated with me. It said, "Life is a one-time offer, use it well!" I remember lying in my bed, reflecting on whether I was using my "one time offer" well. I remember feeling deep pride and satisfaction on how I was using certain areas of my "one time offer." But there were a few areas where I knew I could do better. First, I assessed my relationships. I felt proud that I had deep meaningful connections with my loved ones. I was confident that they all knew how much I loved, cherished, and appreciated them because I made it a practice to not only tell them I loved them, but to also show them. Some of the ways I show my loved ones I love them is by sending them "thinking of you" cards or flowers out of the blue. I support important occasions in their lives by showing up. I am a firm believer in phone calls and have not subscribed to the text only culture that's so popular nowadays. There is something special about hearing a loved one's voice.

Next, I thought about my career. I was less proud of that area. I knew there were certain classes I wanted to take in the area of Happiness Coaching that I had neglected to sign up for. I felt convicted and that same day I signed up for my first Positive Psychology class. I decided that procrastination was not going to cheat me of making the most of my "one time offer." Since then, I have taken numerous classes and even earned a certificate in Positive Psychology Specialization. I have learned so much and have grown tremendously. It has also given me numerous ideas of opportunities to pursue.

Last, I reflected on whether I was surrounding myself with positive energy and experiences. I am happy to report that I was wholly satisfied with that area. This did not magically happen either. A few months earlier, I decided that I was going to prune all the areas that were not bearing fruit out of my life. I consciously disassociated with people or things that were not edifying my life. I had to take inventory. The more I allowed subpar experiences to occupy my life, the less time I devoted to the experiences that were exhilarating, fulfilling, and life enhancing. My rationale then, and still to this day, is that life is short and I have a finite amount of time. And since I am not sure when my "one time offer" will end, I will spend it on the people and things that make my life happier.

If your "one time offer" expired at the end of this month, would you be satisfied with how you've been spending your precious time? Would you refocus your energy on all the people and activities that bring you joy, rather than spend your energy on trivial things, people who mean you no good, and experiences that don't edify you? What do you *really* want? Now assess, what is getting in the way? What daily actions can you take to support creating your dream life?

You are the architect of your own future. If you are not happy with your current situation, change it now! If you live every day as if your "one time offer" is about to expire at the end of the month, I promise you'll live each day more passionately and with more focus and purpose!

Day Twenty-Three

Every storm runs out of rain and the sun will eventually shine again. – Rochelle Gapere

I was talking to a friend of mine and she considerately said to me, "I thought about Tyler every single day for a year after our breakup. During that year I was a bit frustrated with myself for thinking about him so much, but eventually there were days when I wouldn't think about him. And then weeks. And then longer periods. And now I don't think of him at all unless someone mentions him." She was happily relating this to me a few days after her engagement to the love of her life as a way to encourage me that life will go on after heartbreak. I appreciated her candor. I also knew it to be true. I am not sure where I heard the phrase, "every storm runs out of rain," but I modified it to make it my own because I use it to motivate myself during the "stormy" periods of my life.

There is no perfect life! We will all inevitably have rough patches, but it is our perspective during those rough patches that will determine how long it will take us to get through, and how we come out at the other end of the storm. If like me, you adopt the perspective that "eventually the sun will come out again, so while I am in the storm let me weather it," then the inevitable stormy periods of life will become more bearable. I weather the storm by journaling, praying, reading self-development books, and exercising. When the storm seems to be going on much longer than I would imagine, I have to hunker down and remind myself that the sun *will* shine again, and that, this too shall pass! What is your *this* today? Lovingly remind yourself, it shall pass!

The storm analogy is a great metaphor for life, because we have all experienced an extremely rainy day. No matter how dark the sky, no matter how hard the rain fell, and no matter how much lightning lit the sky, it eventually stopped. We were inconvenienced for that day, had to use our rain coats and umbrellas, and probably our rain boots. If your city is anything like Miami, you probably experienced worse traffic than usual because like Miamians, most people don't know how to drive in the rain. However, after all those inconveniences, the rain stopped falling eventually. Maybe during that day you saw a rainbow, and for a split second, seeing that rainbow made you as happy as it usually makes me. The rainbow was a beautiful glimmer of hope during the storm.

As in life, even during the storm there are usually glim -mers of hope, whether a kind word from a friend like mine who shared her testimony to encourage me, or a random act of kindness from a stranger that cheers you up when you feel like you can't possibly go on. When the sun eventually shines in all its glory, you were probably more grateful for the sun than usual.

Similarly with our lives, without the difficult days we wouldn't be as grateful for the peaceful, seamless days. But more to my point, we can assuredly remind ourselves during the storm that the sun *will* shine again, and with that in mind it makes the stormy period of our lives seem more manageable.

Day Twenty—Four

Fight for YOUR happiness, and WIN!
–Rochelle Gapere

In summer 2017, I spent approximately seven weeks in Europe on the adventure of my lifetime thus far. Like I stated earlier, I dubbed it *#RObattical*. One of my dearest friends lives in Oxford, England, so her home was my base. Every few days, as my heart desired, I traveled to a different city. While there, my friend was featured in a British Vogue Magazine article where she was asked to give advice to the upcoming freshman class at Oxford University. One piece of advice resonated with me, "Alongside academic mastery and lifelong connectivity with awesome inspiring people, my biggest take-away from Oxford were lessons in how to fight for happiness. And win." I amended her life advice a tad- Fight for *YOUR* happiness...and WIN!

I believe most people think happiness is elusive and unattainable because they think it should happen without much effort, if at all. Either one is happy or not. However, I beg to differ. Similar to how Mohammed Ali, one of the greatest athletes of all time, practiced and trained diligently and consistently to perfect his boxing skills in order to become one of the best athletes in the sport, we too can practice to add more happiness to our lives. I have learned to exercise my happiness like a muscle. Even when my outer circumstances don't go the way that I want them to – I still choose happiness.

The weeks following the end of my long-term relationship were some of the most challenging moments of my life. Of course, the break up was disappointing, but my life's plans were completely thrown off kilter, as well. Coming to terms with this reality was most difficult. In a season where I had every reason to throw in the towel and wallow in self-pity, I made a conscious decision to do the opposite - I fought for my happiness every day, and most days I won! Each day I would do at least one thing I knew would make me happy. I got to the point where I would wake up with anticipation of what I would be doing to make me happy that day. On the days when I was the saddest, I fought even harder for my happiness.

Those were the days I would take myself to my favorite restaurant to have my favorite meal, or listen to my favorite songs and dance around the house, or watch my favorite funny movies. I committed to doing activities that would be sure to bring me joy and lighten my mood. The more I infused my life with happiness, the happier I became. It wasn't easy. Some days were harder than others, but one thing is for certain, I planned to WIN!

Usually when bad things happen to us we retreat, and

sometimes accept defeat. It is helpful to self-reflect and take the time to learn the lessons that disappointment often provides. However, a bad thing happening to you doesn't mean your entire life is bad. Fighting for your happiness gives you perspective and cultivates gratitude for the good that is happening in the other areas of your life. Yes, I was going through a breakup, but I still had good health, supportive friends and family, and a great career. The more I focused on my happiness in the other areas of my life, the less I focused on the disappointment and heartbreak. The more I fought for my happiness, the less space there was left over for sadness.

Eventually, I woke up one day and wasn't sad or disappointed about the failed relationship anymore. Because I had been prioritizing and fighting for my happiness during that season, I was able to bring new avenues of joy to my life. Things I would take for granted were now at the forefront of my mind. Having to actively fight for my happiness every day strengthened my happiness muscles. That season serves as a great reminder that I don't have to wait for something bad to happen in order to practice happiness every day. Instead, I should commit to doing it every day, in both good and bad seasons. Now, I wake up every day and one of my first thoughts is, "What can I do today that will make me happy?" And I do it!

How will you fight for your happiness and strengthen your happiness muscles to *win*?

Day Twenty-Five

***When life isn't going your way, do you think
God is punishing you? –Rochelle Gapere***

Sometimes when life isn't going our way, we feel like
God is punishing us. However, have you stopped to
think that it's happening the way it is because God has
a bird's eye view of the big picture? For instance, if
you're heading on a road trip from Miami to Orlando
and you get a flat tire in West Palm Beach, of course
it's an inconvenience. In the moment, you'll probably
complain about the delay. If God told you while
changing the tire, "The reason I caused this flat tire is
to prevent an 18 wheeler from cutting you off and
causing a life threatening accident a few exits up,"
then you would be grateful for the delay!

God doesn't have to spell out His entire plan to us. We
just have to learn to trust Him. I always compare God's
care, concern, and love for me to my Mother's. I know
she loves me unconditionally and would never do anything to purposely hurt me. I also know that God loves
me even more than she does. So when life isn't going
my way, I give God the benefit of the doubt. I know
He didn't wake me up this morning thinking "Let me

purposely do something to hurt Rochelle today." If He closes doors, it is because He has greater things in store for us. If you lose a job, it's probably because He wants you to start a business or He has a better job opportunity lined up. If He ends a relationship, it's probably because He has a person that is better suited for you.

Change your mind and perspective when life isn't going your way and give God the benefit of the doubt. I know it is much easier to think of all the bad stuff, but I really want us to practice thinking about all the GOOD stuff. It feels so much better and it makes us happier and more excited about life. When things don't work out, see it as God's protection, not His punishment!

Day Twenty-Six

What do YOU want? Until you get clear about what you want, you will keep attracting experiences or people counter to your desire.
– Rochelle Gapere

What do YOU want? Not what your family wants. Not what your friends want. Not what society tells you to want. What do YOU want? Until you get clear about what you want, you will keep attracting experiences or people counter to your desire.

If you walk into Starbucks and tell the barrister, "I would like a coffee that's sweet and tasty," he will make something that you may or may not like. However, if you ask for a tall skinny vanilla latte then the barrister is clear about the type of coffee you want and will make exactly that. I use that simple example to demonstrate why it is important to have clarity about your desires. I realized that I was giving the Universe mixed signals.

I would say I want a certain outcome, but then I would get things that were sorta-kinda-almost-but not quite like what I thought I wanted. After sitting with myself and focusing my energy inward, I realized I wasn't necessarily being very clear with people about what I truly wanted. I may have started out wanting a certain thing, but as I grew and became more enlightened, I didn't clearly articulate my new desires. Now, I am entirely clear on what I want and more importantly what I need, so I don't entertain anything or anyone counter to that. Your wants will inevitably evolve over time and after different encounters, so it is important that you keep refining them.

You can only get what you ask for, but you will only know what to ask for if you truly take the time to know yourself, your wants, your likes, and your dislikes. How do you get clear about what YOU want? You have to spend quiet time alone where you can tap into the desires of your heart. Ask yourself questions such as: What do I want? WHY do I want that? If I get that, how will that make me feel? How will having that thing help me grow or make me better? If I don't get that thing, what is another alternative? Is the thing I want, the BEST thing for me right now? How will getting what I want contribute to the grandest, highest possible version of myself and my life? You must get clear on your wants, needs, and goals before you can ask others to accommodate them!

Day Twenty-Seven

Not everyone can go where God is taking you. Be comfortable with that fact. Season. Reason. Lifetime. Adjust accordingly. – Rochelle Gapere

I get asked a lot if I'm always happy. To be honest, my natural inclination is to be happy. But I also make a conscious effort to CHOOSE happiness. Case in point: One morning I woke up in a great mood, as I typically do, and eventually checked my WhatsApp. I engaged in conversation with someone I don't speak to often and hadn't heard from in a couple of weeks, and before that, maybe 5 months. Anyhow, the person started becoming passive aggressive with me and tried to sneak in a few underhanded comments. The worst part is that the stuff the person was addressing had happened the year prior. I found myself becoming agitated and then combative.

At that point in my life, I had made a conscious decision to watch my thoughts, words, and interactions to see who or what impacted my energy. As a result, I could feel my energy shifting in a negative way during the conversation. Before I continued the back and forth with the person, I stopped and asked myself if the interaction was positive or negative, and then wrote: "I am in such a different place in my life to be honest.

It's like Michael Jordan talking about his North Carolina days after he won 4 championships. That's me!" I made a conscious decision to rise higher. The person replied: "Good. Well keep on winning. That is what you deserve." I happily moved along and reclaimed my time and energy!

I decided to share this as an example of how you can choose joy, choose happiness, and choose peace. You can't control the actions of others, but you can choose your reaction. To my point, it is absolutely okay to outgrow people, because everyone does not have the capacity to handle where God is taking you.

I have outgrown trying to prove my point to people who are committed to misunderstanding me. That interaction reaffirmed that I am responsible for how long I allow people to occupy space in my life. Whether it's a five minute WhatsApp conversation, or a 2-year relationship, we have the sole responsibility to determine whether an individual is present in our life for a *season, reason* or *lifetime*. Adjust accordingly.

Day Twenty-Eight

Don't let your past delay your destiny. –
Rochelle Gapere

I was talking to a really good friend of mine one evening and we started discussing our 20s and how much fun we had during those years. Eventually the light, lively tone of the conversation changed directions and we started discussing our past mistakes, the lessons learned, and the things we wished we had done better. I told her that even though I wish I could change a few things, I have peace knowing that every experience contributed to the person I am today. Had I chosen a different path back then, my life could be totally different today. Plus, who's to say I'd have preferred that life over the one I have? My friend said she regretted some of the decisions she'd made, and that she would gladly welcome a do over.

I reminded her that the past is gone. It is impossible to relive it or get a chance to do it over. It is important to embrace our past, accept and learn from it, heal what needs to be healed, but then let it go. I am keenly aware that without my past, I wouldn't be the woman I am today. Like my friend, we all have moments where we wish we had done things differently.

However, living in the past is a recipe for frustration, because it is impossible to rewind time. Rather than spend our energy on the impossible, it is more beneficial to use our energy on efforts to improve the present. Living in the past also opens the door for regret to consume us. Regret is also wasted energy. Instead of focusing your attention on the choices you *should have* made, turn your attention to what you can learn and experience in the present. There is power in reflection. When we see how far we have come, it gives us the power and strength to keep pressing toward a brighter future.

There is power in living in the present moment because it is all we have. The longer we dwell on the past, the longer it will take for us to move boldly toward our destiny. We are wiser because of the total sum of our experiences, both good and bad. If we want to be happy we have to let go of what's gone, be grateful for what remains, and look forward to what is coming. Happiness is our birthright! We deserve to wake up every morning excited about life and all its limitless possibilities!

The beauty about the present moment is that we have the power to add or subtract the people, experiences, or things that support our happiness. With the lessons from our past, we are able to make better, wiser, and more well-informed decisions. The sooner we come to terms with our past, the sooner we will be able to live a flourishing and happy present and future.

Day Twenty—Nine

Stop postponing your happiness for a later date.
There is no time like the present to do the things that
make you happy! –Rochelle Gapere

"I will be happy when I get a promotion." "I will be happy when I get married." "I will be happy when I have a baby." "I will be happy when I lose 10 pounds." Do any of these statements sound familiar to you? If yes, why are you postponing your happiness for a later date? Suppose the things that you have conditioned your happiness on never happen, are you prepared to forego your happiness forever? Life is too unpredictable to hold your happiness hostage!

Even Michelle Obama has said that at one point in her life, she postponed her own happiness by placing her needs and wants last. She stated in a Prevention magazine article:

> I have freed myself to put me on the priority list and say, yes, I can make choices that make me happy and that will ripple and benefit my kids, my husband, and my physical health. That's hard for women to own. We're not taught to do that. It's a lesson that I want to

teach my girls so they don't wait for their 'aha' moment until they are in their 30s like I was.

Like Michelle Obama, the sooner you learn to prioritize your happiness, the more beneficial it will be for you and your loved ones.

The thing about postponing our happiness for a later date is that we don't know if or when the conditions we have set in place will happen. Of course, we all need something to look forward to, and be excited about, but our mindset should be, "I am happy with the car I have right now, and I will *also* be happy when I buy my dream car on my vision board." There is no lack of happiness. Happiness is infinite. You can have happiness today and happiness tomorrow and the day after and the day after that. Today, this moment, is the only moment you know you have for sure. Yesterday is gone and tomorrow is not promised. So while you have this moment, make the most of it. Decide today that you will do everything in your power to be happy now.

I too have had to break the habit of postponing things I know will make me happy for a later date. For example, I am fascinated by the Grand Canyon. For some strange reason, I decided that I would wait until I had a family to visit the Grand Canyon. After seeing a picture of the Grand Canyon one morning, I thought to myself, "Why are you waiting for a family to see the Grand Canyon? Suppose that doesn't happen for the next 5 years? Suppose it never happens?" It was pretty silly. I can see the Grand Canyon as a single woman and then see it again if, or when, I have a family. The experience would be different each time, but the thought of seeing it twice invigorated me. I changed my perspective. I still have not visited it as yet, but it is on my to-do list.

I have decided that the things I can do now, I will do now. I know I will be extremely disappointed if I get to the end of my life with a list of things I knew I wanted to do that would have made me happy, but I postponed them to "someday." Living the highest, grandest vision of our lives should be a priority, and we cannot afford to take a gamble on it happening one day!

Day Thirty

We never know where life will take us, or who we will meet along the journey. If we open our hearts with love and kindness to new people and new experiences, the journey will lay pleasant surprises in our path. –
Rochelle Gapere

In September of 2017, Rhodes Trust celebrated its 40 Years of Rhodes Women. The celebratory weekend was held in recognition of Rhodes Trust women, and their achievements across a plethora of sectors and regions. The celebration also marked the 40-year anniversary of the day women became eligible for the scholarship. I had the good fortune of attending a few of the sessions over the weekend, and felt blessed to be in the presence of so many brilliant, strong and determined women who have risen to the pinnacle of their careers through hard work and diligence, and who continue to make significant contributions across the globe.

During one session, I sat with Eden, a young Rhodes Scholar. We chatted for a few minutes afterward, exchanged phone numbers, and made plans to meet.

I firmly believe that life happens exactly as it is supposed to, and that God sends 'God winks' along the journey to confirm that I am on the right path. I first met with Eden at a wine bar, and after just a few moments felt as if I'd known her forever. I advised her about life, love, career, and all things in between. On our second outing at a coffee shop, it was the same – we had great energy and great conversation. While walking home after our meeting that day, I popped into a beautiful cathedral that welcomed passersby in for prayer, a moment of silence, or just time to reflect. I remember sitting in the back of that church and thanking God for clarity of purpose. I had a feeling that I should be a life coach, my Mother and a few close friends had been telling me so for a while, but I hadn't formally acted upon it. I had an 'aha moment' after my time with Eden. By seeing how much the advice I had given her had resonated with her spirit, I knew I was one step closer to solidifying my purpose. It was a 'God wink' that confirmed I was heading in the right direction.

One of the main reasons, I embarked on the *#RObattical* journey was to get clarity about what God wanted me to do next with my life. During the months leading up to my trip, I was in a silent season where I was focusing all my energy inward to ensure that I would make the next right move. I previously had a plan for my life, but thankfully God wrecked my plans before they wrecked me. I trusted God's plans more. Being in Oxford, in a new environment, provided so much clarity.

When I returned to Miami in October 2017, I was clear

sighted and focused as I continued to work on my book. It was an ongoing process of feeling inspired, but then I became distracted by life, work, and travel. I experienced a period during which I was losing momentum. Fortunately, God knows exactly what we need before we need it! In the midst, of the writing lull, I received the most beautiful thank you card from Eden. I received it approximately two months after we'd last seen each other. The timing could not have been more perfect.

Here is the letter she wrote me:

Dear Rochelle,

How can I possibly express my gratitude? I am so fortunate to have met you so serendipitously during your Ro-battical. Though our encounters were few, several elements of your character shone through clearly: you are deeply empathetic, unbelievably confident and resilient, and remarkably profound in how you interpret and navigate the world. In short, you are what many of us (women) aspire tirelessly to be. Thank you for your advice: to know your value, learn your lesson the first time the universe delivers them to you, not take things personally (among the other 3 agreements), and to be clear and resolute with your values.

I am too excited to read your book(s) and even more pleased to receive some of your wisdom first-hand. Most importantly, I hope you continue to create joy for yourself and others as you seem so inclined and able to do! I wish you the best and look forward to keeping in touch.

Warm wishes,
Eden

Eden's letter touched my heart so deeply that it made me cry. The ability to express appreciation is such a beautiful quality. Her letter to me was divine confirmation that I needed to continue writing, and that my purpose was bigger than me. It gave me all the encouragement I needed to finish this book. We never know where life will take us, or who we will meet along the journey, but if we open our hearts with love and kindness to new people and new experiences, the journey will sweetly surprise us. Be kind to each person you encounter, for you never know when that kindness will be returned to inspire you on your God-ordained journey.

Happiness is...*kindness*!

THANK YOU DEAR READER

for accompanying me on the road to happiness. It is my hope that this book will help change your life and shift your perspective on happiness. If this book has impacted you, please share the joy! Encourage your friends and family to experience it too. Your feedback is very important to me. Please leave a review on this book. If you are reading it on amazon kindle, share your thoughts through your kindle reader. If you are flipping through the hard copy, please take a moment to log on to amazon.com to give your review as well.

I wish you HAPPINESS!
Love, Ro

Happiness
is . . .
Kindness!

One Happy Thought At A Time

DAY ONE: *Learn to make happiness enhancing decisions. - Rochelle Gapere*

DAY TWO: *Are you preparing for what you are wishing or hoping for? – Rochelle Gapere*

DAY THREE: *Would 8-year-old you be proud of your current life? –Rochelle Gapere*

DAY FOUR: *Is it worth giving them your joy? – Rochelle Gapere*

DAY FIVE: *Do something today that makes your heart overflow with happiness! – Rochelle Gapere*

DAY SIX: *Be grateful for your portion in life! – Rochelle Gapere*

DAY SEVEN: *Grateful that God woke me up this morning. He didn't have to but He did. And for that, I am beyond thankful. –Rochelle Gapere*

DAY EIGHT: *Maybe it's not working out the way you think it should because God wants to exceed your expectations. –Rochelle Gapere*

DAY NINE: *You honor yourself when you treat yourself well. And you should. –Rochelle Gapere*

DAY TEN: *Focus on your blessings more than your problems! – Rochelle Gapere*

DAY ELEVEN: *Stress is a choice. So is peace. – Unknown*

DAY TWELVE: *Don't get sidetracked by negativity and miss the great things God is about to do in your life. -Rochelle Gapere*

DAY THIRTEEN: *Perspective: Have you ever had a bad day?*

DAY FOURTEEN: *Stop imagining the worst case scenario and use that energy to imagine the BEST case scenario. – Rochelle Gapere*

DAY FIFTEEN: *Do not allow fear to hold you hostage. One brave decision can change your entire life for the better. – Rochelle Gapere*

DAY SIXTEEN: *Protect yourself from emotionally draining interactions by putting buffers in place to preserve your happiness! –Rochelle Gapere*

DAY SEVENTEEN: *Imagine your life 15 years from now! Are you living your life right now in alignment with how you imagine yourself? – Rochelle Gapere*

DAY EIGHTEEN: *Be kind to yourself! Everyone makes mistakes! –Rochelle Gapere*

DAY NINETEEN: *There is supreme power in deliberately tailoring the messaging that infiltrates your thoughts on a daily basis! What can your mind use less of? Try doing away with it and replacing those thoughts with better ones! –Rochelle Gapere*

DAY TWENTY: *Let go off littleness and strive for limitless. –Rochelle Gapere*

DAY TWENTY-ONE: *God is not a one hit wonder. If He did it before, He can certainly do it again. – Rochelle Gapere*

DAY TWENTY-TWO: *While you have life: live it fully, tell & show your loved ones how much you love them, and deflect all bad vibes. –Rochelle Gapere*

DAY TWENTY-THREE: *Every storm runs out of rain and the sun will eventually shine again. – Rochelle Gapere*

DAY TWENTY-FOUR: *Fight for YOUR happiness, and WIN! –Rochelle Gapere*

DAY TWENTY-FIVE: *When life isn't going your way, do you think God is punishing you? –Rochelle Gapere*

DAY TWENTY-SIX: *What do YOU want? Until you get clear about what you want, you will keep attracting experiences or people counter to your desire. – Rochelle Gapere*

DAY TWENTY-SEVEN: *Not everyone can go where God is taking you. Be comfortable with that fact. Season. Reason. Lifetime. Adjust accordingly. – Rochelle Gapere*

DAY TWENTY-EIGHT: *Don't let your past delay your destiny. – Rochelle Gapere*

DAY TWENTY-NINE: *Stop postponing your happiness for a later date. There is no time like the present to do the things that make you happy! – Rochelle Gapere*

DAY THIRTY: *We never know where life will take us, or who we will meet along the journey. If we open our hearts with love and kindness to new people and new experiences, the journey will lay pleasant surprises in our path. –Rochelle Gapere*

ONE **HAPPY THOUGHT** AT A TIME JOURNAL

The *One Happy Thought at a Time Journal* is designed to help you create a plan to live a life that is engaging at every level. It features inspirational quotes and nuggets, as well as, plenty of space to record your thoughts and insights on your journey to becoming the happiest version of you!

While using the *One Happy Thought at a Time Journal* you will be encouraged to:

- *Choose happiness by making happiness enhancing decisions each and every day*
- *Focus your energy on the BEST case scenario*
- *Pre-plan your happiness*
- *Develop a gratitude practice*
- *Fight for your happiness, and win*
- *Evaluate your happiness progress*
- *Reclaim your time and energy from happiness stealers*
- *Infuse your life with happiness on a daily basis*
- *Prepare for what you are wishing or hoping for, so that you can rise to the occasion when the opportunity arises*
- *Master the art of living life fully and passionately*

The One Happy Thought at a Time Journal will become your written record of your happy thoughts! Remember, you have the power to choose *one happy thought* every day, *one happy thought* every hour, or *one happy thought* every minute! The more happy thoughts you choose, I guarantee the result will be a happier you!

6in x 9in portable Journal

AVAILABLE ONLINE

ON AMAZON.COM
AND
WWW.ROCHELLEGAPERE.COM

ROCHELLE GAPERE

is available for coaching sessions, readings and speaking engagements.
To schedule a session or to inquire about an appearance, please visit

www.rochellegapere.com

ABOUT ROCHELLE GAPERE

Rochelle Gapere is an Attorney, Happiness Coach and Entrepreneur. Known for bringing her charismatic personality and sheer joy for living to every experience and individual she encounters, Rochelle has mastered the art of living life fully and passionately. The release of her first book, *One Happy Thought at a Time: 30 Days to a Happier You*, cements her lifelong practice of adding more happiness to this world by empowering others with the tools and techniques that help them lead happier, more fulfilling lives. Rochelle believes in living a life that is engaging at every level and utilizes practical techniques to teach audiences her unique approach to living a happy life.

ABOUT BOOK

In her first book, *One Happy Thought at a Time: 30 Days to a Happier You*, author Rochelle Gapere teaches readers how to live a life that engages them at every level. Through shared personal stories, anecdotes, and life lessons, this book teaches readers how to become a happier version of themselves despite life's inevitable ups and downs.

The lessons in this book will empower readers to make happiness enhancing decisions each and every day.

LET'S CONNECT
ON SOCIAL MEDIA

Facebook
www.facebook.com/rochelle.gapere

Instagram
www.instagram.com/rochelle.gapere

Twitter:
www.twitter.com/rochellegapere

LinkedIn:
www.linkedin.com/in/rochelle-gapere

NOTES

<u>WHAT HAPPY THOUGHTS RESONATED WITH YOU?</u>

_____

_____

_____

_____

_____

_____

_____

_____

_____

_____

_____

_____

_____

_____